Also by Jaroslaw Jankowski

Why Are We So Different?
Your Guide to the 16 Personality Types

Why are we so very different from one another?
Why do we organise our lives in such disparate
ways? Why are our modes of assimilating
information so varied? Why are our approaches
to decision-making so diverse? Why are our
forms of relaxing and 'recharging our batteries'
so dissimilar?

Your Guide to the 16 Personality Types will help you
to understand both yourselves and other people
better. It will aid you not only in avoiding any
number of traps, but also in making the most of
your personal potential, as well as in taking the
right decisions about your education and career
and in building healthy relationships with others.
The book contains the ID16™© Personality
Test, which will enable you to determine your
own personality type. It also offers
a comprehensive description of each of the
sixteen types.

The Artist

Your Guide
to the ISFP Personality Type

The ID16™© Personality Types series

JAROSLAW JANKOWSKI
M.Ed., EMBA

This is a book which can help you exploit your potential more fully, build healthy relationships with other people and make the right decisions about your education and career. However, it should not be considered to be a substitute for expert physiological or psychiatric consultation. Neither the author nor the publisher accept any responsibility whatsoever for any detrimental effects which may result from the inappropriate use of this book.

ID16™© is an independent typology developed by Polish educator and manager Jaroslaw Jankowski and grounded in Carl Gustav Jung's theory. It should not be confused with the personality typologies and tests proposed by other authors or offered by other institutions.

Original title: Twój typ osobowości: Artysta (ISFP)
Translated from the Polish by Caryl Swift
Proof reading: Lacrosse | experts in translation
Layout editing by Zbigniew Szalbot

Published by LOGOS MEDIA

Paperback: ISBN 978-83-7981-057-4
EPUB: ISBN 978-83-7981-058-1
MOBI: ISBN 978-83-7981-059-8

Contents

Preface

The work in your hands is a compendium of knowledge on the *artist*. It forms part of the *ID16™© Personality Types* series, which consists of sixteen books on the individual personality types and *Who Are You? The ID16™© Personality Test*, an introduction to the ID16™© independent personality typology, which is based on the theory developed by Carl Gustav Jung.

As you explore this book on the *artist*, you will find the answer to a number of crucial questions:

- How do *artists* think and what do they feel? How do they make decisions? How do they solve problems? What makes them anxious? What do they fear? What irritates them?
- Which personality types are they happy to encounter on their road through life and

which ones do they avoid? What kind of friends, life partners and parents do they make? How do others perceive them?

- What are their vocational predispositions? What sort of work environment allows them to function most effectively? Which careers best suit their personality type?
- What are their strengths and what do they need to work on? How can they make the most of their potential and avoid pitfalls?
- Which famous people correspond to the *artist*'s profile?

The book also contains the most essential information about the ID16™© typology.

We sincerely hope that it will help you in coming to know yourself and others better.

ID16™© and Jungian Personality Typology

ID16™© numbers among what are referred to as Jungian personality typologies, which draw on the theories developed by Carl Gustav Jung (1875-19161), a Swiss psychiatrist and psychologist and a pioneer of the 'depth psychology' approach.

On the basis of many years of research and observation, Jung came to the conclusion that the differences in people's attitudes and preferences are far from random. He developed a concept which is highly familiar to us today: the division of people into extroverts and introverts. In addition, he distinguished four personality functions, which form two opposing pairs: sensing-intuition and thinking-feeling. He also established that one function is dominant in each pair. He became convinced that each and every person's dominant functions are fixed and independent of external conditions and that, together, what they form is a personality type.

In 1938, two American psychiatrists, Horace Gray and Joseph Wheelwright, created the first personality test based on Jung's theories. It was designed to make it possible to determine the dominant functions within the three dimensions described by Jung, namely, **extraversion-introversion**, **sensing-intuition** and **thinking-feeling**. That first test became the inspiration for other researchers. In 1942, again in America, Isabel Briggs Myers and Katherine Briggs began using their own personality test, broadening Gray's and Wheelwright's classic, three-dimensional model to include a fourth: **judging-perceiving**. The majority of subsequent personality typologies and tests drawing on Jung's theories also take that fourth dimension into account. They include the American typology published by David W. Keirsey in 1978 and the personality test developed in the nineteen seventies by Aušra Augustinavičiūtė, a Lithuanian psychologist. Over the following decades, other European researchers followed in their footsteps, creating more four-dimensional personality typologies and tests for use in personal coaching and career counselling.

ID16™© figures among that group. An independent typology developed by Polish educator and manager Jaroslaw Jankowski, it was published in the first decade of the twenty-first century. ID16™© is based on Carl Jung's classic theory and, like other contemporary Jungian typologies, it follows a four-dimensional path, terming those dimensions the **four natural inclinations**. These inclinations are dichotomous in nature and the picture they provide gives us information regarding a person's personality type. Analysis of the first inclination is intended to determine the dominant **source of life energy**, this being either the exterior or the interior world. Analysis of the second inclination defines the dominant **mode of assimilating information**, which occurs via the senses or via intuition. Analysis of the third inclination supplies a description of the **decision-making mode**, where either mind or heart is dominant, while analysis of the fourth inclination produces a definition of the dominant **lifestyle** as either organised or spontaneous. The combination of all these natural inclinations results in **sixteen possible personality types**.

One remarkable feature of the ID16™© typology is its practical dimension. It describes the individual personality types in action – at work, in daily life and in interpersonal relations. It neither concentrates on the internal dynamics of personality nor does it undertake any theoretical attempts at explaining or commenting on invisible, interior processes. The focus is turned more toward the ways in which a given personality type manifests itself externally and how it affects the surrounding world. This emphasis on the social aspect of personality places ID16™© somewhat closer to the previously mentioned typology developed by Aušra Augustinavičiūtė.

Each of the ID16™© personality types is the result of a given person's natural inclinations.

There is nothing evaluative or judgemental about ascribing a person to a given type, though. No particular personality type is 'better' or 'worse' than any other. Each type is quite simply different and each has its own potential strengths and weaknesses. ID16$^{TM©}$ makes it possible to identify and describe those differences. It helps us to understand ourselves and discover our place in the world.

Familiarity with our personality profile enables us to make full use of our potential and work on the areas which might cause us trouble. It is an invaluable aid in everyday life, in solving problems, in building healthy relationships with other people and in making decisions relating to our education and careers.

Determining personality is a process which is neither arbitrary nor mechanical in nature. As the 'owner and user' of our personality, each and every one of us is fully capable of defining which type we belong to. The individual's role is thus pivotal. This self-identification can be achieved either by analysing the descriptions of the ID16$^{TM©}$ personality types and steadily narrowing down the fields of choice or by taking the short cut provided by the ID16$^{TM©}$ Personality Test.[1] The role played by each 'personality user' is equally crucial when it comes to the test, given that the outcome depends entirely on the answers they provide.

---

[1] The test can be found in *Why Are We So Different? Your Guide to the 16 Personality Types* by Jaroslaw Jankowski.

Identifying personality types helps us to know both ourselves and others. Nonetheless, it should not be treated as some kind of future-determining oracle. No personality type can ever justify our weaknesses or poor interpersonal relationships. It might, however, help us to understand their causes!

ID16™© treats personality type not as a static, genetic, pre-determined condition, but as a product of innate and acquired characteristics. As such, it is a concept which neither diminishes free will nor engages in pigeonholing people. What it does is open up new perspectives for us, encouraging us to work on ourselves and indicating the areas where that work is most needed.

The Artist (ISFP)

THE ID16™© PERSONALITY TYPOLOGY

The Personality in a Nutshell

Life motto: Let's create something!

In brief, *artists* …

… are sensitive, creative and original, with a sense of the aesthetic and natural artistic talents. Independent in character, they follow their own system of values and are optimistic in outlook, with a positive approach to life and an ability to enjoy the moment.

Helping others is a source of joy to them. They find abstract theories tedious and would rather create reality than talk about it, although starting on something new comes more easily to them than finishing what they have already started. They have difficulty in voicing their own desires and needs.

The *artist's* four natural inclinations:

- source of life energy: the interior world
- mode of assimilating information: via the senses
- decision-making mode: the heart
- lifestyle: spontaneous

Similar personality types:

- the Protector
- the Presenter
- the Advocate

Statistical data:

- *artists* constitute between six and nine per cent of the global community
- women predominate among *artists* (60 per cent)
- China is an example of a nation corresponding to the *artist's* profile[2]

The Four-Letter Code

In terms of Jungian personality typology, the universal four-letter code for the *artist* is ISFP.

---

[2] What this means is not that all the residents of China fall within this personality type, but that Chinese society as a whole possesses a great many of the character traits typical of the *artist*.

General character traits

Artists possess a sunny disposition and a refined sense of humour. They follow their own system of values and are insusceptible to external pressure, although the opinion of others also matters a great deal to them. When they evaluate themselves, they do so through the prism of other people's views and assessments of them and, by the same token, are highly sensitive and easily hurt.

Interior compass

Artists have the ability to live for today and enjoy the moment, rarely eating their hearts out over the past or worrying about the future, but living out their lives in the here and now. They love liberty and the sense of freedom; their perception of the world is as a place of limitless possibilities and they are fascinated by its beauty. With their dislike of abstract theories and concepts which are difficult to apply in practice, they would rather experience life than spend time describing it or speculating about it. They strive to live in accordance with the values they hold; acting against their own convictions causes them an enormous sense of uneasiness. The world of the spirit attracts them and, if they profess no particular faith, they tend to be beset by an intense feeling of emptiness, of something lacking.

Healthy relationships with their nearest and dearest are also vital to *artists* and, without them, they are incapable of being happy and enjoying life to the full. They like to live to their own rhythm, finding uniformity and conformity hard to bear.

Unyielding to pressures which affront their principles, they will sometimes have problems with accommodating the prevailing norms and have no liking for bowing to requirements they deem inexplicable, either. They often have a dread of being pigeonholed and restricted and, as a result, will sometimes fear responsibilities and obligations, as well as being concerned that they will lose the chance of being themselves, making their own decisions and choices.

Attitude to others

Artists believe that every person has the right to be themselves, should be accepted as they are and possesses positive potential. They have the ability to spot the good in those who have been rejected and written off by society as a whole. With their uncanny gift for empathy, they are able to help other people, giving them heart and faith in their own powers. They put the needs of others first and express their acceptance of them more or less unconditionally, just so long as their attitude agrees with their own system of values and convictions. They believe that if we all showed one another more love, the world would be a far better place.

They are incapable of understanding people who have a liking for attacking and criticising others and are equally as bewildered by those who flaunt themselves or try to pretend to be something other than they really are, finding the motives for behaviour of that kind incomprehensible. They themselves prize authenticity and exert themselves in the cause of other people's well-being. Endeavouring to make an impression on people is alien to their behavioural repertoire, as is the pursuit of power and influence. They neither impose nor intrude and they make no attempt to exert pressure on others or to persuade them to adopt their own points of view. Sharing their thoughts and reflections is something they do most willingly in the family and among close friends.

As others see them

Other people see *artists* as pleasant, compassionate, calm and modest, but as people who are, nonetheless, difficult to get close to, since they can appear eccentric and mysterious. They themselves are unaware of the fact that this is how they are sometimes perceived. They intrigue those around them because describing and pigeonholing them unequivocally is an elusive affair. In general, they are reserved and withdrawn, although they will sometimes come out of their shell, happily engaging people in conversation and showering them with compliments. At times, they can give the impression of being either flighty or passive, indecisive and bent on avoiding responsibility.

In reality, though, they take life very seriously and, contrary to the opinions of some, are not antisocial, but simply like doing things 'their way', in their own time and at their own pace. They also prefer operating individually to taking part in joint actions and group undertakings of various kinds. Other people will sometimes find their desire to help others hard to understand and, rather than believing that they really are acting without self-interest, seek hidden motives in what they do.

Aesthetics

Artists are usually nature lovers. They have a liking for life in the bosom of nature and adore virgin landscapes, undefiled by civilisation. Aesthetically tuned, they have a feel for beauty and an artistic spirit. They love harmony and natural simplicity and have a superb sense of space, colour, hues and sounds. They are not simply connoisseurs of beauty, but also its creators, possessed of the ability to play with matter and create stunning compositions, images and objects from it. Ever ready and glad to immerse themselves in art, they are often artists … hence the name for this personality type. In general, they are quick to spot new trends in fashion, design and art and, indeed, they are often the trendsetters themselves.

Work style

Artists operate under the sway of the creative impulse, without devoting overmuch time to preparation and deliberation. When an idea pops into their head, they simply go ahead and set about turning it into reality. With their sweeping range of interests, they love turning their hand to trying out something new. Once absorbed in something, they are quite capable of forgetting the entire world, becoming utterly engrossed in their work and losing all track of time. On the other hand, when something else excites their curiosity, they are equally as capable of discarding their current task and giving themselves over completely to the new one.

Artists are highly flexible and capable of adapting to changing circumstances. Their work style often poses something of a puzzle to those around them, since, being easily distracted and having a tendency to immerse themselves in other things, they can give the impression that they fail to make good use of the time they have to carry out their tasks. Despite this, though, they normally manage to meet their deadlines.

Studying

Artists are practical by nature and view theories and concepts which cannot be applied to life as valueless. Rather than theorising on the topic of reality, they prefer to create it.

They often have fairly painful memories of lessons at school. They love learning new things, but find dry, monotonous and theoretical lectures wearisome, learning best and most readily by doing. The very creative process itself is a source of enormous joy to them; indeed, they will often rate it as more important than the end result.

Decisions

When *artists* are solving a problem, they are capable of making a rapid assessment of the situation, taking all the measures and means available to them at the given moment into account and making an on-the-spot decision which meets the occasion. They follow their own system of values and apply a healthy dose of common sense when making their choices. However, reaching a decision analytically and rationally is generally beyond them; as a rule, their consideration of a situation involves thinking about the real people it will affect and about what they will experience and feel. They also reflect on how they themselves will feel if they make this or that decision.

Communication

Artists tend to be reticent, particularly amongst larger groups of people. It may even be that, paralysed by a dread of misunderstanding or criticism, they are frightened of expressing their thoughts openly. As a result, those around them are often unaware of their views, their opinions and their likes and dislikes. In general, they assume that actions speak louder than words, which is why they prefer to convey their feelings and emotions by doing something concrete.

They also have a very low tolerance threshold when it comes to being criticised and, indeed, will often perceive criticism where none was intended. There are times when they may well treat opinions which differ from their own convictions as an attack on their system of values, an attitude which can mean that, on occasion, they will shut out information at variance with their views and thus, in turn, limit their own perceptions.

In the face of stress

To a large extent, *artists'* sense of well-being is dependent on their environment. When surrounded by beauty and harmony, as well as love, warmth and acceptance from others, they are happy, whereas criticism, discord and conflict trigger their sense of being under threat. Their reaction to prolonged periods of stress is to withdraw, give up or escape. Contact with nature and animals has a soothing effect on them, as does immersing themselves in art. As a rule, they love relaxing and unwinding in the open air and have the ability to find joy in the small things in life.

Socially

Artists need space and privacy, which is why they sometimes give the impression of being rather withdrawn and mysterious. Yet their relationships with others are actually of fundamental importance to them and they find it hard to enjoy life if they cannot count on the acceptance and support of those closest to them. They are extraordinarily loyal, take their responsibilities extremely seriously and their friendships are stable and enduring.

In general, they exert themselves in the cause of other people's well-being and will do anything to avoid conflicts. They tread carefully in order not to hurt, distress, sadden or discourage anyone. Although they will happily help others to solve their problems, they distrust people who try to dominate or use them.

Artists are usually reserved towards strangers and take their time in building new acquaintanceships. It is rare for them to express their desires openly and they are reluctant to share their personal problems, an attitude which is often interpreted as a sign that they are distant and withdrawn. Amongst larger groups, they can sometimes be dominated by others, or pushed to the margins or even, quite simply, ignored, which might lead to their becoming embittered and increasingly isolated.

Amongst friends

Artists are seldom numbered among people who have plenty to say for themselves. However, when they do talk to someone, they engage in the conversation to the full, listening attentively and asking questions as and when appropriate, as well as applying their ability to read non-verbal signals. They are genuinely interested in their friends' lives, experiences and personal histories – and they actually remember them! They know who is interested in what and are aware of their likes and dislikes, their passions and their problems. Altruists by nature, they readily hold out a helping hand without ulterior motive; this more often than not takes the form of doing something concrete, rather than talking.

Artists enjoy spending time with like-minded people who accept them for what they are and make no attempt either to change them or to pressurise them. They themselves are both exceptionally tolerant and extremely sensitive to the needs and feelings of others. Faithful and highly devoted, they involve themselves in their relationships wholeheartedly, giving their time and energy to their friends unstintingly. They willingly support others, showing them understanding and providing practical assistance.

They will usually go through their entire lives surrounded by the same group of close friends, amongst whom the most frequently encountered personality types will be *protectors*, *presenters*, *idealists* and other *artists*, while those which feature most rarely will be *directors*, *strategists* and *innovators*.

As life partners

Artists expect trust and understanding from their partners and they themselves also endeavour both to understand them and to respond to their needs. They long for profound relationships and constancy and, at one and the same time, for tolerance and a lack of constraints. Indeed, a mutual respect for the other person's freedom lies at the very core of their relationships.

They seek affirmation of their own worth in their partner's words and gestures. Rarely do they speak of their emotions and feelings; those closest to them are often unaware that, in fact, *artists* are intensely emotional and sensitive people. Always striving for harmony in their relationships and showing their partners immense love and warmth, they, too, have a deep-seated need for endearments, gestures of affection and closeness. When their partner fails to perceive their needs, *artists* may well feel used, superfluous and unattractive. They handle indifference badly and find open criticism even more difficult to cope with, reacting to it by becoming withdrawn and increasingly embittered, as well as by losing all faith in themselves.

The natural candidates for an *artist's* life partner are people of a personality type akin to their own: *protectors*, *presenters* or *advocates*. Building mutual understanding and harmonious relations will be easier in a union of that kind. Nonetheless, experience has taught us that people are also capable of creating happy and successful relationships despite what would seem to be an evident typological incompatibility. Moreover, the differences between two partners can lend added dynamics to a relationship and engender personal development.

As parents

Artists adore children, so the role of parent gives them tremendous joy. They will always find time for their children and every moment with them, every second of fun and every family expedition is something they enjoy to the full. They have an extraordinary and singular bond with their offspring, building it from their earliest years and nurturing it throughout their lives. Their children's individuality is something they respect and they make no attempt to shape them in accordance with their own notions. They will point their children in the right direction, but impose no rigid frameworks, encouraging them to be themselves, pursue their own enthusiasms, live out their own dreams and make the most of their own strengths. In general, *artists* are none too demanding as parents and find it difficult to be tough disciplinarians.

Their flexibility, openness and tolerance may well trigger unlooked-for side effects, since their children sometimes have problems in distinguishing good and desirable behaviour from what is bad and reprehensible. As parents, *artists* are ready to devote their all. As a result, it might be that they spoil their children, fulfilling their every whim and inundating them with presents. Later in life, their offspring appreciate their *artist* parents first and foremost for their acceptance, their warmth and the respect they showed for their decisions and choices.

Work and career paths

Artists can perform a wide range of tasks successfully. However, what gives them the greatest satisfaction is work which enables them to put the values they hold dear into practice. The key to their thriving professionally is their passionate commitment. When they are engaged in something which arouses their enthusiasm, they can move mountains. However, the results they achieve when they find something boring or of little value are somewhat less than impressive and nothing will change that, not even the most remarkable of motivational programmes.

Environment

On the whole, *artists* cope rather less than well in positions demanding that they carry out numerous routine activities and tasks. A formalised environment where everything is bureaucratised, where a host of rigid procedures have to be observed, where detailed guidelines have to be put into practice and where everything has to be done according to plan and within fixed deadlines is torture to them. It is simply not their world.

Artists will often try and plan their careers in a way which means that what they do in life is something which interests them and is important to them. In their case, work is more than a means of earning a living and success is not synonymous with holding a high position and being admired by those around them. They fit in well in institutions where the driving purpose is helping other people and solving their problems and they also enjoy work which offers them contact with nature and animals.

Work style

Artists make for reluctant leaders, since they cope badly when it comes to disciplining people, calling their attention to poor achievements, giving instructions and enforcing duties. They like operating behind the scenes, although this may not always be possible; for instance, if they are artists by profession, they are condemned to being the centre of attention. When they do have to play a leading role, they will get themselves out of the spotlight's glare as quickly as possible.

After they have completed a task, they will happily step back into the shadows. Peace, quiet and time on their own enables them to recharge their batteries and they also have a need for feedback and confirmation that they have done a good job. The opinion of others matters a great deal to them. They themselves tend to be extremely self-critical and to assess what they have done very harshly, often being highly dissatisfied with the results of their work, despite the positive evaluation of those around them.

Other people appreciate *artists* for their practical ideas for solving problems, their flexibility and their improvisational skills when unplanned events and situations crop up without warning. The ability to react rapidly to changing circumstances makes them ideal candidates for rescue work and positions in crisis management centres.

Views on workplace hierarchy

Artists esteem superiors who give their employees freedom, allowing them to be themselves and to carry out their tasks in the way that works best for them. In their opinion, bosses are there to support the people they are in charge of, particularly during difficult moments and crises in people's lives. They like professional relationships to be based on trust and place a high value on a friendly and healthy atmosphere in the workplace. Believing that praise, encouragement and a kind word will achieve more than criticism, discipline and strict supervision, they are happy when their superiors let them know they are satisfied with their work.

On the other hand, they have no liking at all for treating people uniformly or pigeonholing them, and find being told what to do and how they 'should' behave fairly intolerable. By the same token, they themselves neither exert pressure on others nor instruct them, considering that everyone should have the freedom to make their own decisions about their own lives. This approach means that they are unsuited to working in fields where persuasive skills and the ability to pressurise people are a prerequisite, such as jobs involving canvassing for business or soliciting clients, for instance.

Professions

Knowledge of our own personality profile and natural preferences provides us with invaluable help in choosing the optimal path in our professional careers. Experience has shown that, while *artists* are perfectly able to work and find fulfilment in a range of fields, their personality type naturally predisposes them to the following fields and professions:

- artisan
- the arts
- botanist
- chef
- craftsperson
- crisis management
- early primary-level teacher
- fashion designer
- florist
- forester
- gardener
- graphic artist
- hairdresser
- interior decorator
- interior designer
- kindergarten teacher
- lifeguard
- mechanic
- musician
- natural historian
- pet grooming
- photographer

- physician
- psychologist
- social welfare
- stylist
- therapist
- life coach
- travel agent
- vet
- visual artist
- waiter / waitress

Potential strengths and weaknesses

Like any other personality type, *artists* have their potential strengths and weaknesses and this potential can be cultivated in a variety of ways. *Artists'* personal happiness and professional fulfilment depend on whether they make the most of the 'pluses' offered by their personality type and face up to its inherent dangers. Here, then, is a SUMMARY of those 'pluses' and dangers:

Potential strengths

Artists are optimistic by nature, with a positive approach to life. They are exceptionally sincere and are characterised by their openness to people and their tolerance. Being aesthetically inclined, they have a feel for beauty, an artistic spirit and a superb sense of space, colour, hues and sounds, as well as the ability to take whatever tools and materials are available to them and use them to create stunning compositions, images and objects.

They are quicker than most to spot new trends in fashion, design and art. When they are working on tasks they believe in, they are capable of investing enormous effort and energy in them. They learn fast by doing. *Artists* are genuine altruists; they take a sincere interest in other people's experiences and problems and long to help them. They are able to show others warmth and care and respect their individualism. Superb listeners, they will find a positive potential and good in everyone.

With their uncanny gift for empathy, they are able to help other people, giving them heart and faith in their own powers. They are independent, following their own system of values and remaining insusceptible to pressure. Speculations about the future fail to absorb them and worrying over past mistakes is alien to them; they have the ability to focus absolutely on immediate and current problems. Being highly flexible, they find change easy to handle and adapt rapidly to new circumstances, responding to them quickly. They know how to make the most of a situation's potential and, when the need arises, they can improvise brilliantly.

Potential weaknesses

As a rule, *artists* cope none too well with tasks stretching over a lengthy time span and demanding planning, preparation and thinking ahead. Motivating them to do jobs where the results will only become apparent at some distant moment in time is a challenging undertaking. They have a tendency to act and make decisions impulsively and are better at starting something new than at finishing what they have already begun. Analytic and rational decision-making in detachment from real people and situations is difficult for them. In general, they evaluate themselves through the prism of other people's views and assessments of them; by the same token, they are highly sensitive and easily hurt. This might give rise to major problems in the lives of *artists* who are operating in an environment hostile to their nature, for instance among people who are very sparing in their praise or generous in their criticism. They are inclined to have low self-esteem and it is all too easy to undermine their faith in themselves. Openly voicing their thoughts and desires is something they often dread.

Artists have a very low tolerance threshold when it comes to being criticised and may perceive criticism even where none is intended; they are also liable to take opinions which run contrary to their own as an attack on their system of values. This can lead to their shutting out information at variance with their views and limiting their own perceptions as a result. They frequently have problems with assimilating theories and grasping concepts unsuited to practical application. Their individualism and fondness for doing things 'their way' hampers them when it comes to teamwork. When carrying out management functions, they have difficulty in disciplining people, calling their attention to poor achievements, giving instructions and enforcing duties.

Personal development

Artists' personal development depends on the extent to which they make use of their natural potential and surmount the dangers inherent in their personality type. What follows are some practical tips which, together, form a specific guide that we might call *The Artist's Ten Commandments.*

Finish what you start

You launch into new things enthusiastically, but have problems with finishing what you have already started, a *modus operandi* which usually produces mediocre results. Try sorting out what is most important to you and deciding how you want to accomplish it. Then knuckle down and turn your back firmly on all those tempting distractions!

Stop being afraid of conflict

When you find yourself in a situation of conflict, stop hiding your head in the sand and try voicing your point of view and feelings openly instead. Conflict very often helps us to expose problems and solve them.

Don't condemn others to relying on guesswork

Tell people how you feel, what you're going through and what you desire. Stop dithering over whether or not to express your opinions, feelings and emotions and just go for it. You will be helping your colleagues and your nearest and dearest immensely when you do.

Stop fearing ideas and opinions which are different from yours

Before you reject them, give them some consideration and try to understand them. Being open to the viewpoints of others is not synonymous with discarding your own.

Stop fearing criticism

Quell your fear of other people's critical comments. Criticism can be constructive. There is no law which says it has to mean that you are under attack or that your worth is being undermined.

Accept help from others

You operate on the assumption that you should be helping other people and that others seek support from you. Well, when you have a problem, don't hesitate! Ask others for their help and then grasp the hand they offer!

Set yourself free from other people's opinions

You accept others, don't you? So start accepting yourself and stop evaluating yourself on the basis of what other people have to say about you. They could be wrong. They could even be lying. When it comes to making decisions about your life, who could possibly be more competent than you?

Keep your impulsiveness reigned in

Before you make a decision or commit yourself to something, devote a little time to gathering some relevant information, analysing it and evaluating the situation coolly and objectively. That way, you will most probably not only cut down on the number of things you have to do, but will also ensure that you do them more effectively.

Banish those gloomy thoughts

Stop assuming that you are bound to be misunderstood, that you will come a cropper or make a fool of yourself. An attitude to life like that can paralyse you. You will achieve a great deal more by assuming that everything will go swimmingly and focusing on the positive.

Learn to say 'no'

When you disagree with something, why be afraid to say so? Say 'no', particularly when you feel that someone is abusing your help or trying to make you do everything.

Well-known figures

Below is a list of some well-known people who match the *artist's* profile:

- **Wolfgang Amadeus Mozart** (1756-1791); an Austrian composer and musician of the Classical period, one of the three outstanding composers often referred to jointly as the First Viennese School.
- **Fyodor Dostoyevsky** (1821-1881); a Russian writer whose works include *Crime and Punishment*, he is considered one of the world's greatest authors of psychological prose.

- **August François-René Rodin** (1840-1917); a French Symbolist and Impressionist sculptor and precursor of modern sculpture.
- **Vincent van Gogh** (1853-1890); a Dutch painter of the Post-Impressionist school.
- **Marilyn Monroe** (Norma Jean Mortensen/Baker; 1926-1962); an American screen actress and cinema legend whose filmography includes *Some Like It Hot*.
- **Elizabeth Taylor** (1932-2011); a British-American actress whose filmography includes *Cleopatra*, she received numerous awards, including two Oscars.
- **Bob Dylan** (Robert Allen Zimmerman; born in 1941); an American musician, vocalist, composer and writer, he is one of the most important figures in the popular music of the second half of the twentieth century and has won numerous awards, including Grammys, an Oscar and a Pulitzer.
- **Paul McCartney** (born in 1942); an English composer, multi-instrumentalist and songwriter, co-founder of the legendary group the Beatles and holder of numerous prestigious awards.
- **Steven Spielberg** (born in 1946); an American director whose filmography includes *Schindler's List*, he is also a screenwriter and producer and the winner of numerous prestigious awards.

- **Jean Reno** (Juan Morenoy Jederique Jiménez; born in 1948); a French screen actor whose films include *Leon*.
- **Christopher Reeve** (1951-2004); an American actor whose filmography includes the title role in *Superman*, he was also a director and writer.
- **John Travolta** (born in 1954); an American film actor whose movies include *Saturday Night Fever*, he is also a singer and dancer.
- **Kevin Costner** (born 1955); an American actor and director whose filmography includes *Dances with Wolves*, he is also a producer.
- **Earvin 'Magic' Johnson** (born in 1959); a professional American, NBA basketball player and Olympic medallist.

The ID16™© Personality Types in a Nutshell

The Administrator (ESTJ)

Life motto: We'll get the job done!

Administrators are hard-working, responsible and extremely loyal. Energetic and decisive, they value order, stability, security and clear rules. They are matter-of-fact and businesslike, logical, rational and practical and possess the capability to assimilate large amounts of detailed information.

Superb organisers, they are intolerant of ineffectuality, wastefulness and slothfulness. True to their convictions and direct in their contact with others, they present their point of view decisively and openly express critical opinions, sometimes hurting other people as a result.

The *administrator*'s four natural inclinations:

- source of life energy: the exterior world
- mode of assimilating information: via the senses
- decision-making mode: the mind
- lifestyle: organised

Similar personality types:

- the Animator
- the Inspector
- the Practitioner

Statistical data:

- *administrators* constitute between ten and thirteen per cent of the global community
- men predominate among *administrators* (60 per cent)
- the United States is an example of a nation corresponding to the *administrator's* profile[3]

Find out more!

The Administrator. Your Guide to the ESTJ Personality Type by Jaroslaw Jankowski

---

[3] What this means is not that all the residents of the USA fall within this personality type, but that American society as a whole possesses a great many of the character traits typical of the *administrator*.

The Advocate (ESFJ)

Life motto: How can I help you?

Advocates are well-organised, energetic and enthusiastic. Practical, responsible and conscientious, they are sincere and exceptionally gregarious.

Advocates are perceptive of human feelings, emotions and needs. They value harmony and find criticism and conflict difficult to bear. With their sensitivity to any and every manifestation of injustice, prejudice or detriment to another, they are genuinely interested in other people's problems and take real delight in helping them and tending to their needs, while often neglecting their own. They have a tendency to do everything for others and can be vulnerable to manipulation.

The *advocate*'s four natural inclinations:

- source of life energy: the exterior world
- mode of assimilating information: via the senses
- decision-making mode: the heart
- lifestyle: organised

Similar personality types:

- the Presenter
- the Protector
- the Artist

Statistical data:

- *advocates* constitute between ten and thirteen per cent of the global community
- women predominate among *advocates* (70 per cent)
- Canada is an example of a nation corresponding to the *advocate's* profile

Find out more!

The Advocate. Your Guide to the ESFJ Personality Type by Jaroslaw Jankowski

The Animator (ESTP)

Life motto: Let's DO something!

Animators are energetic, active and enterprising. Fond of the company of others, they have the ability to enjoy the moment and are spontaneous, flexible and open to change.

Animators are inspirers and instigators, spurring others to act. Being logical, rational and pragmatic realists, they are wearied by abstract concepts and solutions for the future. Their focus is on solving concrete problems in the here and now. They have difficulties with organising and planning and can be impulsive, acting first and thinking later.

The *animator's* four natural inclinations:

- source of life energy: the exterior world
- mode of assimilating information: via the senses

- decision-making mode: the mind
- lifestyle: spontaneous

Similar personality types:

- the Administrator
- the Practitioner
- the Inspector

Statistical data:

- *animators* constitute between six and ten per cent of the global community
- men predominate among *animators* (60 per cent)
- Australia is an example of a nation corresponding to the *animator's* profile

Find out more!

The Animator. Your Guide to the ESTP Personality Type by Jaroslaw Jankowski

The Artist (ISFP)

Life motto: Let's create something!

Artists are sensitive, creative and original, with a sense of the aesthetic and natural artistic talents. Independent in character, they follow their own system of values and are optimistic in outlook, with a positive approach to life and an ability to enjoy the moment.

Helping others is a source of joy to them. They find abstract theories tedious and would rather create reality than talk about it, although starting on something new comes more easily to them than finishing what they have already started. They have difficulty in voicing their own desires and needs.

The *artist's* four natural inclinations:

- source of life energy: the interior world
- mode of assimilating information: via the senses
- decision-making mode: the heart
- lifestyle: spontaneous

Similar personality types:

- the Protector
- the Presenter
- the Advocate

Statistical data:

- *artists* constitute between six and nine per cent of the global community
- women predominate among *artists* (60 per cent)
- China is an example of a nation corresponding to the *artist's* profile

Find out more!

The Artist. Your Guide to the ISFP Personality Type by Jaroslaw Jankowski

The Counsellor (ENFJ)

Life motto: My friends are my world

Counsellors are optimistic, enthusiastic and quick-witted. Courteous and tactful, they have an extraordinary gift for empathy and find joy in acting for the good of others, with no thought of themselves. They have the ability to influence other people, inspiring them, eliciting their hidden potential and giving them faith in their own powers. Radiating warmth, they draw others to them and often help them in solving their personal problems.

Counsellors can be over-trusting and have a tendency to view the world through rose-tinted glasses. With their focus on other people, they often forget about their own needs.

The *counsellor's* four natural inclinations:

- source of life energy: the exterior world
- mode of assimilating information: intuition
- decision-making mode: the heart
- lifestyle: organised

Similar personality types:

- the Enthusiast
- the Mentor
- the Idealist

Statistical data:

- *counsellors* constitute between three and five per cent of the global community
- women predominate among *counsellors* (80 per cent)
- France is an example of a nation corresponding to the *counsellor's* profile

Find out more!

The Counsellor. Your Guide to the ENFJ Personality Type by Jaroslaw Jankowski

The Director (ENTJ)

Life motto: I'll tell you what you need to do.

Directors are independent, active and decisive. Rational, logical and creative, when they analyse problems they look at the wider picture and are able to foresee the future consequences of human activities. They are characterised by optimism and a healthy sense of their own worth and are capable of transforming theoretical concepts into concrete, practical plans of action.

Visionaries, mentors and organisers, *directors* possess natural leadership skills. Their powerful personalities and direct and critical style can often have an intimidating effect, causing them problems in their interpersonal relationships.

The *director's* four natural inclinations:

- source of life energy: the exterior world

- mode of assimilating information: intuition
- decision-making mode: the mind
- lifestyle: organised

Similar personality types:

- the Innovator
- the Strategist
- the Logician

Statistical data:

- *directors* constitute between two and five per cent of the global community
- men predominate among *directors* (70 per cent)
- Holland is an example of a nation corresponding to the *director's* profile

Find out more!

The Director. Your Guide to the ENTJ Personality Type by Jaroslaw Jankowski

The Enthusiast (ENFP)

Life motto: We'll manage!

Enthusiasts are energetic, enthusiastic and optimistic. Capable of enjoying life and looking ahead to the future, they are dynamic, quick-witted and creative. They have a liking for people in general, value honest and genuine relationships and are warm, sincere and emotional. Criticism is something they handle badly. With their gift for empathy and ability to perceive people's needs, feelings and motives, they both inspire others and infect them with their own enthusiasm.

They love to be at the centre of events and are flexible and capable of improvising. Their inclination leads towards idealistic notions. Being easily distracted, they have problems with seeing things through to the end.

The *enthusiast's* four natural inclinations:

- source of life energy: the exterior world
- mode of assimilating information: intuition
- decision-making mode: the heart
- lifestyle: spontaneous

Similar personality types:

- the Counsellor
- the Idealist
- the Mentor

Statistical data:

- *enthusiasts* constitute between five and eight per cent of the global community
- women predominate among *enthusiasts* (60 per cent)
- Italy is an example of a nation corresponding to the *enthusiast's* profile

Find out more!

The Enthusiast. Your Guide to the ENFP Personality Type by Jaroslaw Jankowski

The Idealist (INFP)

Life motto: We CAN live differently.

Idealists are sensitive, loyal, and creative. Living in accordance with the values they hold is of immense importance to them and they both manifest an interest in the reality of the spirit and delve deeply into the mysteries of life. Wrapped up in the world's problems and open to the needs of other people, they prize harmony and balance.

Idealists are romantic; not only are they able to show love, but they also need warmth and affection themselves. With their outstanding ability to read other people's feelings and emotions, they build healthy, profound and enduring relationships. They feel that they are on very shaky ground in situations of conflict and have no real resistance to stress and criticism.

The *idealist's* four natural inclinations:

- source of life energy: the interior world
- mode of assimilating information: intuition
- decision-making mode: the heart
- lifestyle: spontaneous

Similar personality types:

- the Mentor
- the Enthusiast
- the Counsellor

Statistical data:

- *idealists* constitute between one and four per cent of the global community
- women predominate among *idealists* (60 per cent)
- Thailand is an example of a nation corresponding to the *idealist's* profile

Find out more!

The Idealist. Your Guide to the INFP Personality Type by Jaroslaw Jankowski

The Innovator (ENTP)

Life motto: How about trying a different approach…?

Innovators are inventive, original and independent. Optimistic, energetic and enterprising, they are people of action who love being at the centre of events and solving 'insoluble' problems. Their thoughts are turned to the future and they are curious about the world and visionary by nature. Open to new concepts and ideas, they enjoy new experiences and experiments and have the ability to identify the connections between separate events.

Innovators are spontaneous, communicative and self-assured. However, they tend to overestimate their own possibilities and have problems with seeing things through to the end. They are also inclined to be impatient and to take risks.

The *innovator's* four natural inclinations:

- source of life energy: the exterior world
- mode of assimilating information: intuition
- decision-making mode: the mind
- lifestyle: spontaneous

Similar personality types:

- the Director
- the Logician
- the Strategist

Statistical data:

- *innovators* constitute between three and five per cent of the global community
- men predominate among *innovators* (70 per cent)
- Israel is an example of a nation corresponding to the *innovator's* profile

Find out more!

The Innovator. Your Guide to the ENTP Personality Type by Jaroslaw Jankowski

The Inspector (ISTJ)

Life motto: *Duty first.*

Inspectors are people who can always be counted on. Well-mannered, punctual, reliable, conscientious and responsible, when they give their word, they keep it. Being analytical, methodical, systematic and logical by nature, they tend be seen as serious, cold and reserved. They prize calm, stability and order, have no fondness for change and like clear principles and concrete rules.

Inspectors are hard-working, persevering and capable of seeing things through to the end. As perfectionists, they try to exercise control over everything within their sphere and are sparing in their praise. They also underrate the importance of other people's feelings and emotions.

The *inspector's* four natural inclinations:

- source of life energy: the interior world
- mode of assimilating information: via the senses
- decision-making mode: the mind
- lifestyle: organised

Similar personality types:

- the Practitioner
- the Administrator
- the Animator

Statistical data:

- *inspectors* constitute between six and ten per cent of the global community
- men predominate among *inspectors* (60 per cent)
- Switzerland is an example of a nation corresponding to the *inspector's* profile

Find out more!

The Inspector. Your Guide to the ISTJ Personality Type by Jaroslaw Jankowski

The Logician (INTP)

Life motto: Above all else, seek to discover the truths about the world.

Logicians are original, resourceful and creative. With a love for solving problems of a theoretical nature, they are analytical, quick-witted, enthusiastically disposed towards new concepts and have the ability to connect individual phenomena, educing general rules and theories from them. Logical, exact and inquiring, they are quick to spot incoherence and inconsistency.

Logicians are independent, sceptical of existing solutions and authorities, tolerant and open to new challenges. When immersed in thought, they will sometimes lose touch with the outside world.

The *logician's* four natural inclinations:

- source of life energy: the interior world

- mode of assimilating information: intuition
- decision-making mode: the mind
- lifestyle: spontaneous

Similar personality types:

- the Strategist
- the Innovator
- the Director

Statistical data:

- *logicians* constitute between two and three per cent of the global community;
- men predominate among *logicians* (80 per cent)
- India is an example of a nation corresponding to the *logician's* profile

Find out more!

The Logician. Your Guide to the INTP Personality Type by Jaroslaw Jankowski

The Mentor (INFJ)

Life motto: The world CAN be a better place!

Mentors are creative and sensitive. With their gaze fixed firmly on the future, they spot opportunities and potential imperceptible to others. Idealists and visionaries, they are geared towards helping people and are conscientious, responsible and, at one and the same time, courteous, caring and friendly. They strive to understand the mechanisms governing the world and view problems from a wide perspective.

Superb listeners and observers, *mentors* are characterised by their extraordinary empathy, intuition and trust of people and are capable of reading the feelings and emotions of others. They find criticism and conflict difficult to bear and can come across as enigmatic.

The *mentor's* four natural inclinations:

- source of life energy: the interior world
- mode of assimilating information: intuition
- decision-making mode: the heart
- lifestyle: organised

Similar personality types:

- the Idealist
- the Counsellor
- the Enthusiast

Statistical data:

- *mentors* constitute one per cent of the global community and are the most rarely occurring of the sixteen personality types
- women predominate among *mentors* (80 per cent)
- Norway is an example of a nation corresponding to the *mentor's* profile

Find out more!

The Mentor. Your Guide to the INFJ Personality Type by Jaroslaw Jankowski

The Practitioner (ISTP)

Life motto: Actions speak louder than words.

Practitioners are optimistic and spontaneous, with a positive approach to life. Reserved and independent, they hold true to their personal convictions and view external principles and norms with scepticism. They find abstract concepts and solutions for the future tiresome and would far rather roll up their sleeves and get to work on solving tangible and concrete problems.

Adapting well to new places and situations, they enjoy fresh challenges and risks and are capable of keeping a cool head in the face of threats and danger. Their general reticence and extreme reserve when it comes to expressing their opinions mean that other people may often find them impenetrable.

The *practitioner's* four natural inclinations:

- source of life energy: the interior world
- mode of assimilating information: via the senses
- decision-making mode: the mind
- lifestyle: spontaneous

Similar personality types:

- the Inspector
- the Animator
- the Administrator

Statistical data:

- *practitioners* constitute between six and nine per cent of the global community
- men predominate among *practitioners* (60 per cent)
- Singapore is an example of a nation corresponding to the *practitioner's* profile

Find out more!

The Practitioner. Your Guide to the ISTP Personality Type by Jaroslaw Jankowski

The Presenter (ESFP)

Life motto: Now is the perfect moment!

Presenters are optimistic, energetic and outgoing, with the ability to enjoy life and have fun to the full. Practical, flexible and spontaneous at one and the same time, they enjoy change and new experiences, coping badly with solitude, stagnation and routine.

With their liking for being at the centre of attention, they are natural-born actors and their speaking abilities arouse the interest and enthusiasm of their listeners. Focused as they are on the present moment, they will sometimes lose sight of their long-term aims and can also have problems with foreseeing the consequences of their actions.

The *presenter's* four natural inclinations:

- source of life energy: the exterior world
- mode of assimilating information: via the senses
- decision-making mode: the heart
- lifestyle: spontaneous

Similar personality types:

- the Advocate
- the Artist
- the Protector

Statistical data:

- *presenters* constitute between eight and thirteen per cent of the global community
- women predominate among *presenters* (60 per cent)
- Brazil is an example of a nation corresponding to the *presenter's* profile

Find out more!

The Presenter. Your Guide to the ESFP Personality Type by Jaroslaw Jankowski

The Protector (ISFJ)

Life motto: Your happiness matters to me.

Protectors are sincere, warm-hearted, unassuming, trustworthy and extraordinarily loyal. With their ability to perceive people's needs and their desire to help them, they will always put others first. Practical, well-organised and gifted with both an eye and a memory for detail, they are responsible, hard-working, patient, persevering and capable of seeing things through to the end.

Protectors set great store by tranquillity, stability and friendly relations with others and are skilled at building bridges between people. By the same token, they find conflict and criticism difficult to bear. Given their powerful sense of duty and their constant readiness to come to the aid of others, they can end up being used by people.

The *protector's* four natural inclinations:

- source of life energy: the interior world
- mode of assimilating information: via the senses
- decision-making mode: the heart
- lifestyle: organised

Similar personality types:

- the Artist
- the Advocate
- the Presenter

Statistical data:

- *protectors* constitute between eight and twelve per cent of the global population
- women predominate among *protectors* (70 per cent)
- Sweden is an example of a nation corresponding to the *protector's* profile

Find out more!

The Protector. Your Guide to the ISFJ Personality Type by Jaroslaw Jankowski

The Strategist (INTJ)

Life motto: I can certainly improve this.

Strategists are independent and outstandingly individualistic, with an immense seam of inner energy. Creative, inventive and resourceful, others perceive them as competent, self-assured and, at one and the same time, distant and enigmatic. No matter what they turn their attention to, they will always look at the bigger picture and they have a driving urge to improve the world around them and set it in order.

Well-organised, responsible, critical and demanding, they are difficult to knock off balance – and just as hard to please to the full. Reading the emotions and feelings of others is something they find very problematic.

The *strategist's* four natural inclinations:

- source of life energy: the interior world
- mode of assimilating information: intuition
- decision-making mode: the mind
- lifestyle: organised

Similar personality types:

- the Logician
- the Director
- the Innovator

Statistical data:

- *strategists* constitute between one and two per cent of the global community
- men predominate among *strategists* (80 per cent)
- Finland is an example of a nation corresponding to the *strategist's* profile

Find out more!

The Strategist. Your Guide to the INTJ Personality Type by Jaroslaw Jankowski

Additional information

The four natural inclinations

1. THE DOMINANT SOURCE OF LIFE
   ENERGY

   a. THE EXTERIOR WORLD
      People who draw their energy
      from outside. They need activity
      and contact with others and find
      being alone for any length of time
      hard to bear.

   b. THE INTERIOR WORLD
      People who draw their energy
      from their inner world. They need
      quiet and solitude and feel drained

when they spend any length of time in a group.

2. THE DOMINANT MODE OF ASSIMILATING INFORMATION

    a. VIA THE SENSES
    People who rely on the five senses and are persuaded by facts and evidence. They have a liking for methods and practices which are tried and tested and prefer concrete tasks and are realists who trust in experience.

    b. VIA INTUITION
    People who rely on the sixth sense and are driven by what they 'feel in their bones'. They have a liking for innovative solutions and problems of a theoretical nature and are characterised by a creative approach to their tasks and the ability to predict.

3. THE DOMINANT DECISION-MAKING MODE

    a. THE MIND
    People who are guided by logic and objective principles. They are critical and direct in expressing their opinions.

b. THE HEART
People who are guided by their feelings and values. They long for harmony and mutual understanding with others.

4. THE DOMINANT LIFESTYLE

a. ORGANISED
People who are conscientious and organised. They value order and like to operate according to plan.

b. SPONTANEOUS
People who are spontaneous and value freedom of action. They live for the moment and have no trouble finding their feet in new situations.

The approximate percentage of each personality type in the world population

Personality Type:	Proportion:
• The Administrator (ESTJ):	10-13%
• The Advocate (ESFJ):	10-13%
• The Animator (ESTP):	6-10%
• The Artist (ISFP):	6-9%
• The Counsellor (ENFJ):	3-5 %
• The Director (ENTJ):	2-5%
• The Enthusiast (ENFP):	5-8%

- The Idealist (INFP):   1-4%
- The Innovator (ENTP):   3-5%
- The Inspector (ISTJ):   6-10%
- The Logician (INTP):   2-3%
- The Mentor (INFJ):   ca. 1%
- The Practitioner (ISTP):   6-9%
- The Presenter (ESFP):   8-13%
- The Protector (ISFJ):   8-12%
- The Strategist (INTJ):   1-2%

The approximate percentage of women and men of each personality type in the world population

Personality Type:	Women / Men:
The Administrator (ESTJ):	40% / 60%
The Advocate (ESFJ):	70% / 30%
The Animator (ESTP):	40% / 60%
The Artist (ISFP):	60% / 40%
The Counsellor (ENFJ):	80% / 20%
The Director (ENTJ):	30% / 70%
The Enthusiast (ENFP):	60% / 40%
The Idealist (INFP):	60% / 40%
The Innovator (ENTP):	30% / 70%
The Inspector (ISTJ):	40% / 60%
The Logician (INTP):	20% / 80%
The Mentor (INFJ):	80% / 20%
The Practitioner (ISTP):	40% / 60%
The Presenter (ESFP):	60% / 40%
The Protector (ISFJ):	70% / 30%
The Strategist (INTJ):	20% / 80%

Bibliography

- Arraj, Tyra & Arraj, James: *Tracking the Elusive Human, Volume 1: A Practical Guide to C.G. Jung's Psychological Types, W.H. Sheldon's Body and Temperament Types and Their Integration*, Inner Growth Books, 1988

- Arraj, James: *Tracking the Elusive Human, Volume 2: An Advanced Guide to the Typological Worlds of C. G. Jung, W.H. Sheldon, Their Integration, and the Biochemical Typology of the Future*, Inner Growth Books, 1990

- Berens, Linda V.; Cooper, Sue A.; Ernst, Linda K.; Martin, Charles R.; Myers, Steve; Nardi, Dario; Pearman, Roger R.; Segal, Marci; Smith, Melissa: *A Quick Guide to the 16 Personality Types in Organizations: Understanding Personality Differences in the Workplace*, Telos Publications, 2002

- Geier, John G. & Downey, E. Dorothy: *Energetics of Personality*, Aristos Publishing House, 1989
- Hunsaker, Phillip L. & Alessandra, Anthony J.: *The Art of Managing People*, Simon and Schuster, 1986
- Jung, Carl Gustav: *Psychological Tyspes (The Collected Works of C. G. Jung, Vol. 6)*, Princeton University Press, 1976
- Kise, Jane A. G.; Stark, David & Krebs Hirsch, Sandra: *LifeKeys: Discover Who You Are*, Bethany House, 2005
- Kroeger, Otto & Thuesen, Janet: *Type Talk or How to Determine Your Personality Type and Change Your Life*, Delacorte Press, 1988
- Lawrence, Gordon: *People Types and Tiger Stripes*, Center for Applications of Psychological Type, 1993
- Lawrence, Gordon: *Looking at Type and Learning Styles*, Center for Applications of Psychological Type, 1997
- Maddi, Salvatore R.: *Personality Theories: A Comparative Analysis*, Waveland, 2001
- Martin, Charles R.: *Looking at Type: The Fundamentals Using Psychological Type To Understand and Appreciate Ourselves and Others*, Center for Applications of Psychological Type, 2001
- Meier C.A.: Personality: *The Individuation Process in the Light of C. G. Jung's Typology*, Daimon Verlag, 2007

- Pearman, Roger R. & Albritton, Sarah: *I'm Not Crazy, I'm Just Not You: The Real Meaning of the Sixteen Personality Types*, Davies-Black Publishing, 1997

- Segal, Marci: Creativity and Personality Type: *Tools for Understanding and Inspiring the Many Voices of Creativity*, Telos Publications, 2001

- Sharp, Daryl: Personality Type: *Jung's Model of Typology*, Inner City Books, 1987

- Spoto, Angelo: *Jung's Typology in Perspective*, Chiron Publications, 1995

- Tannen, Deborah: *You Just Don't Understand*, William Morrow and Company, 1990

- Thomas, Jay C. & Segal, Daniel L.: *Comprehensive Handbook of Personality and Psychopathology, Personality and Everyday Functioning*, Wiley, 2005

- Thomson, Lenore: *Personality Type: An Owner's Manual*, Shambhala, 1998

- Tieger, Paul D. & Barron-Tieger Barbara: *Just Your Type: Create the Relationship You've Always Wanted Using the Secrets of Personality Type*, Little, Brown and Company, 2000

- Von Franz, Marie-Louise & Hillman, James: *Lectures on Jung's Typology*, Continuum International Publishing Group, 1971

Putting the Reader first.

An Author Campaign Facilitated by ALLi.

www.ingramcontent.com/pod-product-compliance
Lightning Source LLC
Chambersburg PA
CBHW031208020426
42333CB00013B/846